Psychologist

CAREERS WITH CHARACTER

Careers with Character

Psychologist

by Shirley Brinkerhoff

MASON CREST PUBLISHERS

Mason Crest Publishers Inc.
370 Reed Road
Broomall, Pennsylvania 19008
(866) MCP-BOOK (toll free)
www.masoncrest.com

First printing
1 2 3 4 5 6 7 8 9 10
Library of Congress Cataloging-in-Publication Data on file at the Library of Congress.
ISBN 1-59084-322-3
        1-59084-327-4 (series)

Design by Lori Holland.
Composition by Bytheway Publishing Services, Binghamton, New York.
Printed and bound in the Hashemite Kingdom of Jordan.

Photo Credits:
Artville: pp. 4, 7, 8, 16, 18, 20, 21, 46, 50, 54, 84
Corbis: pp. 56, 82, cover
Corel: p. 10
Digital Stock: p. 80
Eyewire: pp. 13, 24, 44, 47, 49, 67
PhotoDisc: pp. 22, 26, 28, 29, 30, 31, 34, 36, 37, 39, 43, 48, 57, 58, 65, 68, 72, 75, 77
Viola Ruelke Gommer: pp. 62, 64

CONTENTS

We each leave a fingerprint on the world.
Our careers are the work we do in life.
Our characters are shaped by the choices
we make to do good.
When we combine careers with character,
we touch the world with power.

INTRODUCTION

by Dr. Cheryl Gholar
and Dr. Ernestine G. Riggs

In today's world, the awesome task of choosing or staying in a career has become more involved than one would ever have imagined in past decades. Whether the job market is robust or the demand for workers is sluggish, the need for top-performing employees with good character remains a priority on most employers' lists of "must have" or "must keep." When critical decisions are being made regarding a company or organization's growth or future, job performance and work ethic are often the determining factors as to who will remain employed and who will not.

How does one achieve success in one's career and in life? Victor Frankl, the Austrian psychologist, summarized the concept of success in the preface to his book *Man's Search for Meaning* as: "The unintended side-effect of one's personal dedication to a course greater than oneself." Achieving value by responding to life and careers from higher levels of knowing and being is a specific goal of teaching and learning in "Careers with Character." What constitutes success for us as individuals can be found deep within our belief system. Seeking, preparing, and attaining an excellent career that aligns with our personality is an outstanding goal. However, an excellent career augmented by exemplary character is a visible expression of the human need to bring meaning, purpose, and value to our work.

Career education informs us of employment opportunities, occupational outlooks, earnings, and preparation needed to perform certain

1

tasks. Character education provides insight into how a person of good character might choose to respond, initiate an action, or perform specific tasks in the presence of an ethical dilemma. "Careers with Character" combines the two and teaches students that careers are more than just jobs. Career development is incomplete without character development. What better way to explore careers and character than to make them a single package to be opened, examined, and reflected upon as a means of understanding the greater whole of who we are and what work can mean when one chooses to become an employee of character?

Character can be defined simply as "who you are even when no one else is around." Your character is revealed by your choices and actions. These bear your personal signature, validating the story of who you are. They are the fingerprints you leave behind on the people you meet and know; they are the ideas you bring into reality. Your choices tell the world what you truly believe.

Character, when viewed as a standard of excellence, reminds us to ask ourselves when choosing a career: "Why this particular career, for what purpose, and to what end?" The authors of "Careers with Character" knowledgeably and passionately, through their various vignettes, enable one to experience an inner journey that is both intellectual and moral. Students will find themselves, when confronting decisions in real life, more prepared, having had experiential learning opportunities through this series. The books, however, do not separate or negate the individual good from the academic skills or intellect needed to perform the required tasks that lead to productive career development and personal fulfillment.

Each book is replete with exemplary role models, practical strategies, instructional tools, and applications. In each volume, individuals of character work toward ethical leadership, learning how to respond appropriately to issues of not only right versus wrong, but issues of right versus right, understanding the possible benefits and consequences of their decisions. A wealth of examples is provided.

What is it about a career that moves our hearts and minds toward fulfilling a dream? It is our character. The truest approach to finding out who we are and what illuminates our lives is to look within. At the very heart of career development is good character. At the heart of good character is an individual who knows and loves the good, and seeks to share the good with others. By exploring careers and character together, we create internal and external environments that support and enhance each other, challenging students to lead conscious lives of personal quality and true richness every day.

Is there a difference between doing the right thing, and doing things right? Career questions ask, "What do you know about a specific career?" Character questions ask, "Now that you know about a specific career, what will you choose to do with what you know?" "How will you perform certain tasks and services for others, even when no one else is around?" "Will all individuals be given your best regardless of their socioeconomic background, physical condition, ethnicity, or religious beliefs?" Character questions often challenge the authenticity of what we say we believe and value in the workplace and in our personal lives.

Character and career questions together challenge us to pay attention to our lives and not fall asleep on the job. Career knowledge, self-knowledge, and ethical wisdom help us answer deeper questions about the meaning of work; they give us permission to transform our lives. Personal integrity is the price of admission.

The insight of one "ordinary" individual can make a difference in the world—if that one individual believes that character is an amazing gift to uncap knowledge and talents to empower the human community. Our world needs everyday heroes in the workplace—and "Careers with Character" challenges students to become those heroes.

Psychologists open doors into the human mind.

1

JOB REQUIREMENTS

Psychology has a long past,
but only a short history.
—Hermann Ebbinghaus
(early experimental psychologist)

Jennifer was terrified of birds. So terrified, in fact, that she could no longer go to work. Her office building was located beside the city park, where pigeons flocked in great number. Jennifer had tried to approach her building from all different directions, but it seemed she always saw at least one pigeon, a sight that terrified her and left her shaking. Her fear was so intense that sometimes she was unable to run away or even walk.

"I have no idea why I'm like this," Jennifer confessed to the psychologist. "I don't even know when the fear started. I just remember one spring break when I was in college, and my friends and I all went to Florida. There were seagulls all over the beaches, and they made me uneasy. But I don't know why. I'd been to the beach lots of times with my family, and I loved the gulls—I even fed them bread.

"All I know is, I've got to get rid of the fear, or I'm going to lose my job!"

Jennifer's psychologist explained that Jennifer had a bird *phobia*. He set up a program of *behavior therapy*, in which Jennifer would act out a *systematic desensitization* to unlearn her fear of birds. Gradually, over a period of many weeks, she was exposed under controlled circumstances to:

- watching another woman about her own age (the model) touch bird pictures;
- touching the bird pictures with the model;
- touching the pictures on her own;
- watching the model touch a stuffed bird from a museum;
- touching the stuffed bird, first with gloves on, and later without them.

Then Jennifer was taught to fight off birds by waving her arms and shouting, first by watching the model do it, then by trying these actions on a group of pigeons at the park. Next, Jennifer and the model visited a live-poultry store where they touched baby chicks; then a zoo with a duck pond, an aviary, and cages for large birds. At last, Jennifer was able to walk through the large, closed-in aviary, where she was surrounded

For a person with a phobia, even something as innocuous as a turkey farm may look as terrifying as a scene from Hitchcock's horror film, The Birds.

When individuals are suffering under a dark cloud of depression and anxiety, psychologists offer a "life saver."

by scores of birds, and eventually even moved to a waterfront apartment where she frequently encountered gulls. At Jennifer's 12-month follow-up visit to the psychologist, her bird phobia had not returned.

When two planes collided over San Diego several years ago, killing 144 people, police and firemen were the first on the scene. There they faced the horrible effects of the crash, which included body parts and tissue scattered over a wide areas of houses, lawns, and roads. The officers who had to identify and label the bodies later experienced severe stress symptoms, including nightmares, insomnia, headaches, memory loss, and gastrointestinal problems. Some of the officers actually found themselves paralyzed when they tried to put on the uniform they'd been wearing on the day of the accident.

Although some of the officers at first felt "unmanly" to be so upset and to ask for help, psychologists were able to help them overcome their stress reactions in numerous ways:

- They prescribed active ways for the officers to work out their frustration and anger, including jogging and target shooting.
- They used ***behavior modification*** techniques to help officers deal with the ***amnesia*** about the disaster.
- They found that simply providing empathy and understanding, as well as reassuring the officers that they were normal to have these problems in such an abnormal situation, was the most successful treatment of all.

Psychologists help people in the ways described in the previous examples, but their field includes many other situations as well. Psychology is the study of the behavior of organisms, and attempts to describe, explain, and predict that behavior. Psychologists may study an animal's brain to understand eating disorders; research which colors of emergency dashboard lights are most visible to astronauts; stay awake all night observing people in a sleep study; study the effects of activity on

Some psychologists study sleep disorders.

the health of zoo animals; observe the behavior of infants to discover what behaviors are "normal" at different ages; and much more.

How did psychology begin? What does it take to become a psychologist?

Modern psychology can be said to have begun just a little over a century ago, with a German named Wilhelm Wundt, the first person known to call himself a psychologist. Wundt founded the first formal laboratory for experimental psychology, and soon other such labs appeared in North America, usually in universities. The first in the United States, opened in 1883, was at Johns Hopkins University. By 1900 there were more than 40 of these labs. Edward Titchener, who had a laboratory at Cornell University, was one of the first psychologists in the United States.

Ideas from philosophy and natural science both contributed to the development of psychology. In 1890, William James, a Harvard philosophy professor with strong interests in medicine, literature, and religion, wrote the two-volume *The Principles of Psychology*, which is considered by many to be the most important psychology text of all. In 1892, the American Psychological Association was founded.

When psychology is mentioned, many people think first of **psychoanalysis**, a form of **psychotherapy**, and of its founder, Sigmund Freud. In 1895, Freud discovered that some problems simply went away when people talked about them. From this information, he developed the idea of a "talking cure," and immediately began dig-

> ### Excerpt from the American Psychiatric Association's Ethics Code
>
> *Psychologists work to develop a valid and reliable body of scientific knowledge based on research. They may apply that knowledge to human behavior in a variety of contexts. In doing so, they perform many roles, such as researcher, educator, diagnostician, therapist, supervisor, consultant, administrator, social interventionist, and expert witness. Their goal is to broaden knowledge of behavior, and, where appropriate, to apply it pragmatically to improve the condition of both the individual and society. . . .*

Why a Couch?

Why do many people automatically think of a couch with a therapist sitting beside or behind it when they hear about psychoanalysis or psychotherapy? Sigmund Freud first developed this idea. He like to have patients recline on a couch, then sat behind them, removing his physical presence far enough away from them so that **transference** became easier. He believed this was a way to gain insight into the thought processes of his patients, observing the transference of their feelings from a parent or lover to a therapist.

Today most psychologists do not use a couch; instead, they talk with clients across a desk or in an informal living-room setting.

ging deeper into this concept. He studied how the human personality worked and why talking to other humans helped. As people became aware of Freud's report that special kinds of conversations could relieve problems medicine couldn't touch, his idea of a talking cure caught on. The central idea of psychoanalysis was that certain unhealthy psychological processes (unrecognized by and hidden from the patient) were the source of their problems. The talking cure could be used to figure out these psychological processes and to help the unconscious dynamics become conscious, allowing patients to work through the unhealthy patterns and replace them with healthier, intentional approaches to handling life.

Many new schools of thought grew out of Freud's discoveries. Some psychologists agreed with his ideas. Others departed from them radically. One of the main criticisms of the original form of psychoanalysis was the length—and thus the cost—of the treatment. Freud felt that patients should have therapy sessions three to five times a week, possibly for as long as six years. This idea has given rise to many jokes. In Woody Allen's movie *Sleeper*, Allen is placed in suspended animation for 2,000 years. When he revives and discovers how long he's been asleep, he says, "My analyst was a strict Freudian. If I'd been going to him all this time I'd almost be cured now."

Although psychotherapy may be the best known branch of psychology, it is only one part of a very broad field. A doctorate in psychology (Ph.D. or Psy.D.) is necessary for most people who make psychology their career. Those with a Ph.D. qualify for teaching, research, clinical, and counseling positions in elementary and secondary schools, universities, private industry, and government. Those with the Psy.D. usually work in clinical positions. Those who have a master's degree in school psychology or an Ed.S. (Educational Specialist) degree can work as school psychologists. There are positions available to people with a master's degree, such as industrial-organizational psychologist, but these positions typically neither pay as well nor offer the responsibility of positions open to those with a doctorate.

With a bachelor's degree, a person may assist psychologists in community mental health centers, vocational rehabilitation offices, and correctional programs; or work as research or administrative assistant. He or she may also work in sales or in related fields such as marketing research.

Preparation for a career in psychology should include a college preparatory course in high school, with a concentration on English courses. During graduate work, math and sciences are also valuable. Reading comprehension of French and German is one of the usual requirements for the doctoral degree.

Psychology has at least 40 areas of specialization, as listed by the American Psychological Association (APA). Following are a few of these areas, with a short summary of what each involves:

- **Experimental psychologists** examine the fundamental processes governing behavior. They often conduct their research in a laboratory and investigate sensation, perception, learning, memory, motivation, and other related areas.
- **Physiological and comparative psychologists** study the effects of biological factors on behavior. Physiological psychologists study the brain, nervous system, genes, and drugs, all in relation to behavior. Comparative psychologists look at behavioral differences and similarities between species.
- **Developmental psychologists** study the development and change of common human behaviors, including language, social attachments, emotions, thinking, and perception.
- **Social psychologists** examine the effects people have on each other, including cooperation, aggression, affection, group pressure, altruism, and similar topics.
- **Clinical psychologists** focus on understanding, diagnosing, and treating abnormal or *deviant* behaviors. This group is the largest division of psychology, and its practitioners usually work in counseling centers, independent or group practices, hospitals, or clinics. Some clinical psychologists provide individual, family, or group psychotherapy, designing and implementing treatment and intervention programs. Others work in medical schools, training

students to deliver mental health and behavioral medicine services.

- **School psychologists** work in the schools to resolve students' learning and behavior problems, collaborating with teachers, parents, and other school personnel. They also work with students who have disabilities, or gifted and talented students, and may evaluate the effectiveness of academic programs and behavior management procedures.
- **Industrial** or **organizational psychologists** work on improving working conditions, production rates, and decision-making abilities in the business world.
- **Educational psychologists** focus on the learning process, including teaching methods, curricula, and making learning easier and more efficient.

School psychologists work in schools to help students learn.

- **Counseling psychologists** help individuals solve problems not stemming from serious mental disorders. Examples would include academic and vocational problems.

Although a strong educational background is necessary to succeed in psychology, it is not the only requirement for becoming a psychologist. Emotional stability and maturity, the ability to work effectively with people, and good communication skills are also essential. Patience and perseverance are vital, because psychological treatments and research both usually take a long time. Many of the positive character qualities necessary to be a successful psychologist are covered in the following chapters, including:

- integrity and trustworthiness
- respect and compassion
- justice and fairness
- responsibility
- courage
- self-discipline and diligence
- citizenship

Few other professions provide the opportunity to relate so closely to other people and to help in such a wide variety of situations. As a result, good character is a vital requirement for this profession.

Intelligence plus character—that is the true goal of education.

—Martin Luther King, Jr.

Psychology can provide an "umbrella" that helps protects families from the effects of emotional disorders.

2

INTEGRITY AND
TRUSTWORTHINESS

*Being a person of integrity means far more
than simply avoiding dishonesty. Deciding
when to offer the truth—and to whom—
requires careful thought.*

Steve Preston folded his cell phone closed and dropped it back into his shirt pocket.

"Something wrong?" Julie asked.

Steve glanced across the patio table at his wife, who was stretched out on a lounge chair in the afternoon sunshine, and shrugged noncommittally. *Nothing I can discuss with you,* he thought. *Or anyone else, for that matter.*

For the next hour, as he watched his twin daughters splash and dive in the pool and made quiet conversation with Julie, he tried to figure out what to do. The call had come from his secretary. She had just been contacted by the Domestic Relations Department, and they were looking for information about one of his patients.

As a psychologist, Steve knew he was duty-bound to report certain things. Child abuse, for instance. No question there. Or a patient who threatened to shoot the President—no question about that one, either.

So why are real-life cases seldom that simple? Steve wondered.

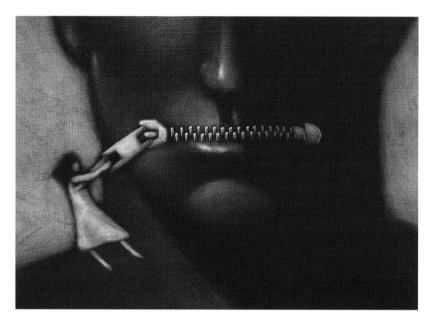

A psychologist with integrity often faces ethical dilemmas about when to preserve a patient's right to confidentiality—and when to speak out.

Integrity (The American Psychiatric Association's Ethics Code)

Psychologists seek to promote integrity in the science, teaching, and practice of psychology. In these activities psychologists are honest, fair, and respectful. In describing or reporting their qualifications, services, products, fees, research, or teaching, they do not make statements that are false, misleading, or deceptive. Psychologists strive to be aware of their own belief systems, values, needs, and limitations and the effect of these on their work. To the extent feasible, they attempt to clarify for relevant parties the roles they are performing and to function appropriately in accordance with those roles. Psychologists avoid improper and potentially harmful dual relationships.

Nothing in the Ethics Code that he could think of said specifically that he had to answer questions from the Domestic Relations Department about whether or not his patient, Thomas Corona, was gambling on the Internet.

Thomas, a top executive in a large electronics firm in Hartford, had first come to Steve's office just a year ago, scared because his sporadic gambling trips to Atlantic City had recently expanded to include sports and animal betting. He was losing so much money that meeting his child support payments was becoming almost impossible. He had to have help, he told Steve.

Steve guided him in setting up some accountability relationships, and together they drew up a structured daily activity plan that was helping Thomas get control of his behavior. Then someone introduced Thomas to Internet gambling. Overnight, all the progress he'd made seemed to disappear. Within a few months, he was thousands of dollars in arrears on child support.

> People who value integrity and trustworthiness:
>
> • tell the truth.
> • don't withhold important information.
> • are sincere; they don't deceive, mislead, try to trick others.
> • don't betray a trust.
> • don't steal.
> • don't cheat.
> • stand up for beliefs about right and wrong.
> • keep their promises.
> • return what they have borrowed and pay their debts.
> • support and protect their families, friends, community, and country.
> • don't talk behind people's backs or spread rumors.
> • don't ask their friends to do something wrong.
>
> Adapted from material from the Character Counts Coalition, 4640 Admiralty Way, Suite 1001, Marina del Rey, California 90292.

Once again, Steve began working with Thomas on the basics of responsibility and self-control. Thomas was deeply ashamed. "If anybody ever found out about my gambling—besides you, I mean—I don't know how I could go on," he frequently told Steve. "My whole life would be over."

Thomas started making progress again, but not as much as before.

The four enemies of integrity:

- self-interest (The things we want . . . the things we might be tempted to lie, steal, or cheat to get.)
- self-protection (The things we don't want . . . the things we'd lie, steal, or cheat to avoid.)
- self-deception (When we refuse to see the situation clearly.)
- self-righteousness (When we think we're always right . . . an end-justifies-the-means attitude.)

Adapted from materials from the Josephson Institute of Ethics, 4640 Admiralty Way, Suite 1001, Marina del Rey, California 90292.

Because the Internet gambling was so readily available around the clock, seven days a week, it was much harder to control than a trip to Atlantic City.

However, Steve also knew that Thomas's former wife was unable to work because she was in the middle of chemotherapy for advanced breast cancer. She desperately needed regular child support payments, especially right now. As Steve looked at his own little girls, screaming and splashing each other in the pool, he wondered if Thomas's kids had enough to eat; if Thomas's irresponsible behavior was contributing negatively to his former wife's health struggles. In a

When the needs of two individuals conflict, a trustworthy psychologist must weigh the options objectively, without being influenced by financial gain or other selfish motivations.

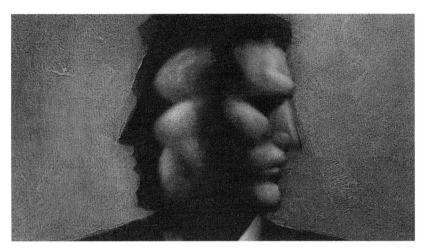

A person with integrity is not two-faced!

Three Foundations for Ethical Decision-Making

1. Take into account the interests and well-being of everyone concerned. (Don't do something that will help you if it will hurt another.)
2. When a character value like integrity and trustworthiness is at stake, always make the decision that will support that value. (For example, tell the truth even though it may cost you some embarrassment.)
3. Where two character values conflict (for instance, when telling the truth might hurt another person), choose the course of action that will lead to the greatest good for everyone concerned. Be sure to seek all possible alternatives, however; don't opt for dishonesty simply as the easiest and least painful way out of a difficult situation.

Adapted from materials from the Josephson Institute of Ethics, 4640 Admiralty Way, Suite 1001, Marina del Rey, California 90292.

Compulsive gambling is a disorder that can harm both individuals and families.

way, Thomas's behavior was hurting his kids as surely as child abuse, and therapy was proceeding very slowly.

If Steve divulged what he knew, Thomas might have to appear before Judge Hatfield, known for the hard line he took on "dead-beat dads." Thomas could be ordered to participate in a program for gambling addicts; he could even be incarcerated, which might only make the situation worse. On the other hand, the threat of an appearance before Judge Hatfield might spur Thomas to evaluate his behavior and cooperate more fully with his therapy.

Steve's phone rang and he checked the caller ID. It was his secretary again. He knew he'd have to make a decision. He just wasn't sure what it should be.

Honesty is better than all policy.

—Immanuel Kant

High school should be a safe, happy world—and psychologists are working to make that ideal a reality.

3

RESPECT AND COMPASSION

[People] are respectable only
as they respect.
—Ralph Waldo Emerson

On April 20, 1999, Eric Harris and Dylan Klebold gunned down 12 students and one teacher at Columbine High School in Colorado before they turned their guns on themselves and committed suicide.

The Columbine shooting was one in a long list of school shootings that have occurred in the United States. Many people wondered then, and continue to wonder, what could have motivated this kind of violence, and psychologists are studying the subject intently. Suggestions as to a cause range from growing up in dysfunctional homes to being bullied at school, but one possible explanation came up again and again in conjunction with the Columbine shootings: repeated exposure to violence in video games, television programs, and movies.

Some experts emphatically reject the idea that viewing violence could influence or motivate violent behavior on the part of viewers. Other experts disagree.

Social learning by observation and imitation is an efficient learning method, and obviously occurs in many areas of life. If all human learning had to be done by trial and error, imagine how long it would take to master even the simplest of tasks. But can violence be learned by viewing others committing violence?

One study of social learning, now considered a classic, was done by Albert Bandura at Stanford University in 1963. Bandura arranged to have nursery school children observe an adult striking a large, inflated Bobo doll with a mallet. The adult also hit, kicked, and sat on the doll, and verbalized several unusual sentences while doing so. Later, the children were observed while they played in a room filled with toys, including the Bobo doll. Children who had not seen the adult's behavior were also included in this setting. The children who had observed the adult's aggressive behavior toward the doll were far more likely to be aggressive toward it than the other children. Many of them also imitated the unusual verbal statements made by the adult.

Bandura set up another study in 1965, in which one group of children watched as a model was rewarded with juice and candy for being aggressive. Other children observed the model being scolded for the same aggression. Those who observed the model being rewarded for aggressive behavior became more aggressive. Those who observed the model being scolded rarely imitated the model's behavior.

Psychologists study how groups of children behave in different settings.

After Columbine, the wife of slain teacher Dave Sanders filed a lawsuit blaming violent movies and video games for propelling Harris and Klebold into their deadly rampage, but the suit was dismissed by U. S. District Judge Lewis Babcock on March 5, 2002. Judge Babcock's opinion was that the law generally does not impose responsibility on a person to foresee the intentional violent acts of others and that movies, video games, and other forms of visual art are components of a society dedicated to free expression.

According to an article in the *Denver Post* on March 5, 2002, the judge said, "The court flatly reject(s) the notion that society is better served by insulating the vulnerable from exposure. . . . To shield children . . . from exposure to violent descriptions and images would not only be quixotic, but deforming; it would leave them unequipped to cope with the world as we know it."

People who value respect and compassion:

- are courteous and polite.
- are tolerant; they accept individual's differences.
- don't mistreat or make fun of anyone.
- don't use or take advantage of others.
- respect others' rights to make their own decisions.
- are sensitive to others' feelings.
- live by the Golden Rule. (They treat others the way they want to be treated.)
- help others.
- share what they have with others.
- do what they can to help those who are in trouble.
- forgive others.

Adapted from material from the Character Counts Coalition, 4640 Admiralty Way, Suite 1001, Marina del Rey, California 90292.

Within just a few weeks of the above decision, results of a 17-year study on TV's effects on violence, by psychologist Jeffrey G. Johnson of Columbia University and the New York State Psychiatric Institute, were published. Though short-term studies on the subject had been done before, this was the first long-term study that investigated total TV watching time and then followed the subjects over many years, controlling for other contributing factors to violence. More than 1,000 families in the Albany and Saratoga counties of New York started the study, and

Children learn respect from others by imitating the words and actions of the adults in their lives.

Respect (the American Psychiatric Association's Ethics Code)

Psychologists accord appropriate respect to the fundamental rights, dignity, and worth of all people. They respect the rights of individuals to privacy, confidentiality, self-determination, and autonomy, mindful that legal and other obligations may lead to inconsistency and conflict with the exercise of these rights. Psychologists are aware of cultural, individual, and role differences, including those due to age, gender, race, ethnicity, national origin, religion, sexual orientation, disability, language, and socioeconomic status. Psychologists try to eliminate the effect on their work of biases based on those factors, and they do not knowingly participate in or condone unfair discriminatory practices.

reports on over 700 of them were done at the end (some people moved away or dropped out). Results showed that teens (especially teen boys) who watch more than an hour of television a day during early adolescence are more likely to be violent in later years. Violence in this report included assaults, fights, and robberies. The rate of violence was seen to increase fivefold if daily TV viewing time was extended to three or more hours.

Although girls were included in this study, boys showed the most dramatic increase in involvement in violence. Of all those who watched less than an hour of TV

> **Respect for the Feelings of Others**
>
> Among those who stand,
>   do not sit;
> among those who sit,
>   do not stand.
> Among those who laugh,
>   do not weep;
> among those who weep,
>   do not laugh.
>   —Jewish proverb

Teenage violence may be caused in part by the prevalence of violence in television shows and video games.

Learning Respect at Home

If violence can be a learned behavior, does the same hold true for respect and compassion?

While parents find a certain amount of fighting between siblings inevitable, there are times when they must intervene with what Dr. Haim Ginott terms "a loud and clear statement" of values. He suggests the following statements:

- Mimicking is not allowed.
- Hurting is absolutely forbidden.
- There will be no torture in this house.
- No one may deliberately tease another person to tears.
- People are not for hurting.
- People are for respecting.

From *Between Parent and Teenager,* by Dr. Haim Ginott (Toronto, Ont.: Macmillan, 1969).

Respect and compassion are character qualities that need to be nurtured in the home.

Families benefit when they turn off the television and have fun together.

per day at age 14, around six were later (by the ages of 16 to 22) involved in aggressive acts. Of those who watched between one and three hours of TV, the rate increased to 22.5, and to 28.8 percent for those who watched more than three hours. For boys, however, the rates were 8.9 percent for those watching less than one hour, 32.5 percent for those watching one to three hours, and 45.2 percent for those watching more than three hours.

On the basis of his study findings, Johnson commented in a March 28, 2002 Associated Press article, "Our findings suggest that, at least during early adolescence, responsible parents should avoid permitting their children to watch more than one hour of television a day." The American Psychological Association, American Academy of Pediatrics, American Medical Association, and other such organizations have also reported connections between viewing violent TV programs and aggressive behavior.

Another psychologist immediately attributed the results of this study to observer bias, which holds that the observer's conclusions are skewed by what he or she wishes to see. The debate continues on this as on many other issues, but one important function that psychologists perform in our society is to provide information for each of us to use in making our own decisions.

For instance, imagine that you are the parent of two elementary school-aged boys who are fascinated by video games. Your mother-in-law buys them a video game, which they happily play for two hours while you get some much needed time talking with your spouse. That night, before you go to bed, you decide to have a closer look at the video game. As you play it, you discover that the main character is required to shoot and kill, or at least maim, as many other characters as possible in order to win the title of "Hero." Not only is he not punished for hurting and killing, he is actually rewarded for it.

Your spouse refuses to get involved, telling you not to "make a big deal of it." What will you do? Throw away the game? Try to talk your sons out of playing it altogether? Limit their time playing it? Substitute a different game more in line with the goals of respecting and having compassion for all people?

Nothing good ever comes of violence.

—Martin Luther

The elderly in our society deserve to be treated with justice and fairness.

4

JUSTICE AND FAIRNESS

Keep thyself then . . . a friend of justice.
—Marcus Aurelius Antoninus

When Pat Moore decided to research **ageism**, she disguised herself as an 85-year-old woman. She inserted clouded contact lenses that diminished her vision, and earplugs to make her hearing less acute. Bindings on her legs made walking difficult, as it is for many elderly people; taping her fingers gave her the diminished **dexterity** of a person with arthritic hands. Then she went out into society to see how people would respond to her.

As a "little old lady," Moore struggled to survive in our society, which is by and large designed for those who are young, strong, and agile. Opening jars, holding pens, reading labels, or climbing up bus steps all posed difficulty for her. Even more disturbing, few people offered her help when she needed it. She was ridiculed for being old and vulnerable. Once she was even violently attacked by a gang of adolescents.

What would make people treat an elderly person in this way? Clues to the basis of ageism may be found in greeting cards that bemoan our advancing age, in the less-than-positive portrayal of the elderly on TV and in advertisements, and in the language our society uses to describe older people: geezer, old fogey, old maid, dirty old man, and old goat. Businesses often show reluctance to hire or promote older workers. In some sectors, there is still an enforced retirement age.

An elderly person often faces prejudice.

Beneath these practices lie attitudes that are really myths and ***stereotypes*** about aging. Here are just three of those myths:

- Many people believe that the elderly are sick far more frequently than younger people, when in fact 78 percent of those 65 and over are healthy enough to engage in all their normal activities. While those over 65 have more chronic illnesses, they have less acute illnesses, fewer injuries in the home, and fewer highway accidents than younger people.
- Some people believe that old people are ugly. In American culture, youth is associated with beauty, and older people, especially women, face terms such as crone, fossil, goat, hag, witch, withered, wizened, wrinkled. But the idea that age equals ugliness is purely cultural; it has no foundation in reality, and other cultures look at aging differently. In some European cultures, for example, older women are considered "sexier," and

These older individuals have lives as satisfying and rewarding as any younger person.

in Japan, silver hair and wrinkles are admired as signs of wisdom and maturity.

- Older people are sometimes thought to have lost their usefulness, but studies of those employed under actual working conditions show they perform as well as, if not better than, younger workers on most measures. Their consistency of output often increases with age; older workers have less job turnover, fewer accidents, and less absenteeism than younger workers.

People who value justice and fairness:

- treat all people the same (as much as possible).
- are open-minded; they are willing to listen to the points of views of others and try to understand.
- consider carefully before making decisions that affect others.
- don't take advantage of others' mistakes.
- don't take more than their fair share.
- cooperate with others.
- recognize the uniqueness and value of each individual.

Adapted from material from the Character Counts Coalition, 4640 Admiralty Way, Suite 1001, Marina del Rey, California 90292.

Stereotypes are dehumanizing and promote one-dimensional thinking. Stereotyped elders are not seen as humans but as objects, and therefore, can more easily be denied rights. Psychologists study this sort of thinking. As a result, they are able to see past it. They realize that devaluing one segment of our population is contrary to our American values, which entail respect for human worth and dignity. Such devaluation also causes a vital human resource to be lost, in that the elderly are often wrongfully considered "unemployable."

Psychologists perform studies such as the one Pat Moore did in order to let the truth be known about older people. Only when the stereotypes are dispelled will people be treated with the fairness and justice they deserve.

Justice and Fairness
(the American Psychiatric Association's Ethics Code)

Psychologists seek to contribute to the welfare of those with whom they interact professionally. In their professional actions, psychologists weigh the welfare and rights of their patients or clients, students, supervisees, human research participants, and other affected persons, and the welfare of animal subjects of research. When conflicts occur among psychologists' obligations or concerns, they attempt to resolve these conflicts and to perform their roles in a responsible fashion that avoids or minimizes harm. Psychologists are sensitive to real and ascribed differences in power between themselves and others, and they do not exploit or mislead other people during or after professional relationships.

In our society, judges help determine what is legally fair.

Older people have much to offer younger people.

How Do You Feel About Age and Aging?

Exploring our own attitudes about older people is the first step to changing ageism. The following questions are from a quiz developed by Barrie Robinson, MSSW, School of Social Welfare, University of California at Berkeley, 1994.

1. When is a person "old"?
2. When will you be "old"?
3. How should you refer to a person who is "old"? How will you want others to refer to you when you are "old"?
4. What special entitlements, if any, should "old" people receive just because of their age?
5. Lists some changes we will experience as we become "old"?
6. What are the worst and best parts of growing older?

What Is Your Aging I.Q.?

True or False?

1. Most people will become "senile" sooner or later if they live long enough.
   False. Only 20-25 percent of all elderly people develop **Alzheimer's disease** or other brain disease. Less then 10 percent are disoriented or demented. . . . **Dementia** or memory loss is not a normal part of aging, but typically indicates some organic condition.
2. Intelligence declines with age.
   False. Most people maintain their intellect or improve as they grow older. It may take longer to learn something new; reaction times may slow. But this does not impair the ability to reason and function well.
3. Most elderly have little interest in or capacity for sexual relations.
   False. The majority continue to have both the interest and capacity well into their 70s, 80s, and even 90s.
4. American families, by and large, have abandoned their elderly members.
   False. The American family is still the number-one caretaker of older members. Most older persons live close to their children. Eight out of 10 older men and six out of 10 older women live in family settings.
5. Aged drivers have more accidents than younger drivers.
   False. Per person, drivers over 65 have fewer accidents than those under 65.

6. Personality changes with age, just like hair color and skin texture.

   False. Personality doesn't change with age. Therefore, all old people cannot be described as rigid or opinionated, only those who always were.

7. All five senses decline with age.

   True. But the extent of the changes varies greatly among individuals.

8. The elderly naturally withdraw from participation in community life in advanced old age.

   False. Although this theory was once accepted, it has generally now been discredited.

9. Hearing loss is the third most common chronic condition for the elderly.

   True. After arthritis and heart disease, hearing loss is the most common chronic disorder reported in the elderly population.

Source: Barrie Robinson, MSSW, School of Social Welfare, University of California at Berkeley, 1994. A variety of sources were used, including *Age-Wave: The Challenges and Opportunities of Our Aging America* by Ken Dychtwald and Joe Flower; *Why Survive? Being Old in America* by Robert Butler; "Facts on Aging Quiz" by Erdman B. Palmore; and "What Is Your Aging IQ?" published by the National Institute on Aging.

Civilization is first of all a moral thing. Without truth, respect for duty, love of neighbor and virtue, everything is destroyed. The morality of a society is alone the basis of civilization.

—Henri Frederic Amiel

Psychologists can help ease the difficult years of adolescence.

5

RESPONSIBILITY

*Controlling our negative emotions is one of
our hardest responsibilities.*

Susan Helman opened the trunk of the car, took one look at the spoiled groceries inside, and gagged. The pork chops were pale and warm to the touch, the ten-pound value pack of hamburger was a sickly brown. The entire mess smelled putrid. Susan felt a wave of fury sweep over her, as she slammed open the door that led from the garage to the kitchen.

"Jason? JASON!"

There was no answer from her 14-year-old son, and Susan mentally armed herself with ammunition for the confrontation as she strode through the kitchen. All she had asked of him—two days ago—was to unload the groceries and put them away. How hard could it be to unload a few bags of groceries? And who was going to pay for $35.00 worth of spoiled meat? Not her, that was for sure.

Susan rounded the corner of the family room and stopped dead. There sat Jason zapping electronic aliens on the computer screen, his head bobbing rhythmically to whatever was streaming through those high-tech headphones, absolutely oblivious to what he'd done. *Again.*

If you were Susan Helman, what would you feel was your responsibility in this situation? What positive result would you most want from a confrontation with 14-year-old Jason?

What would be the best way to achieve that result? In what ways could achievement of that result be derailed? What tools could you use to cope with your sudden anger to best achieve the positive result?

If you were Jason, how would you most want your mother to deal with you? How would you least want her to deal with you?

Fortunately, a few months before Susan found the spoiled meat, she had accepted responsibility for her own emotions, including her feelings of frustration and anger at her son. She decided she'd had enough of these angry confrontations with her son Jason. She was tired of the cycle they were in: her anger at Jason led her to say harmful words to him, which caused her to feel deep regret and shame at having spoken to him that way. Finally, she would make awkward attempts at reconciliation. Each time they went through this cycle, she could sense Jason moving farther and farther away from her emotionally. Susan had grown desperate to stop the deterioration in their relationship, but she found that when she tried to hold in or ignore her anger, it only led to bigger blow-ups later on. As the adult in the relationship, she knew she was responsible for

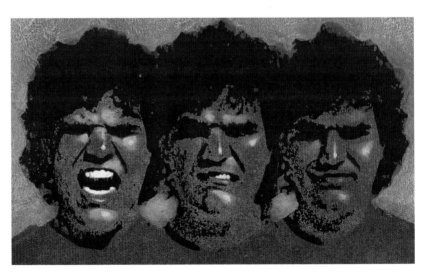

Psychology offers people help with anger management.

Anger can often act as a barrier between children and their parents.

Taking Responsibility for Anger

Dr. Haim Ginott, a psychologist who helps parents relate to children, addresses the anger some parents feel, particularly during their children's teen years. He recommends that parents deal with their stress by recognizing these facts:

1. We accept the fact that in the natural course of events teenagers will make us uncomfortable, annoyed, irritated, angry, and furious.
2. We are entitled to these feelings without guilt, regret, or shame.
3. We are entitled to express our feelings, with one limitation. No matter how angry we are, we do not insult teenagers' personality and character.

Adapted from *Between Parent and Teenager,* by Dr. Haim G. Ginott (New York: Macmillan, 1969).

As people of character, we need to take responsibility for our anger, rather than blaming the other person for our emotions.

People who value responsibility:

- think before they act; they consider the possible consequences of their actions.
- accept responsibility for the consequences of their choices.
- don't blame others for their mistakes or take credit for others' achievements.
- don't make excuses.
- set a good example for others.
- pursue excellence in all they do.
- do the best with what they have.
- are dependable; others can rely on them.

Adapted from material from the Character Counts Coalition, 4640 Admiralty Way, Suite 1001, Marina del Rey, California 90292.

creating more positive interactions with her son.

Susan had begun looking for someone to help her find a better way to interact with her son by checking out books from the public library. There she found the writings of psychologists such as Dr. Haim Ginott, who specialized in parent-child relationships. The turning point in her relationship with Jason came when she read Dr. Ginott's advice about accepting anger.

Thanks to psychologists like Dr. Ginott, Susan discovered that, instead of trying to suppress her anger, she could take responsibility to express it in nondestructive ways.

Write It Down

Usually, time is an ally when we are battling strong negative emotions. People feel what can seem to be an overwhelming need to express those emotions immediately, but when they do so, much damage can be done to relationships and to individuals. Another option is to write those feelings down and then wait to evaluate what's been written until the strong emotions have calmed down. This is one good way to take responsibility for your own emotions. Writing can include letters, journal entries, or lists (of feelings, of possible steps to solutions, etc.). Writing can then be laid aside for later consideration and action.

A blank book or notebook and a pen can be helpful tools for coping with angry feelings.

We may sometimes feel we are walking an emotional tightrope, especially during adolescence. Psychology offers techniques that can help us balance ourselves more smoothly.

By expressing her anger without insulting or damaging Jason, she could get her point across and not create feelings of resentment or revenge in him. This gave Susan the relief of expressing her anger, while still helping Jason gain insight into the effects of his actions.

Through books, as well as through one-on-one counseling, psychologists help people like Susan take responsibility for their relationships, their emotions, and their interactions with others. Psychologists' professional skills are powerful tools for building communities where individuals value responsibility.

> ### Dealing with Sudden Anger
>
> Describe what you see.
> Describe what you feel.
> Describe what needs to be done.
> Do not attack the person.
>
> Adapted from *Between Parent and Teenager,* by Dr. Haim G. Ginott

---

Accepting Responsibility
(the American Psychiatric Association's Ethics Code)

Psychologists uphold professional standards of conduct, clarify their professional roles and obligations, accept appropriate responsibility for their behavior, and adapt their methods to the needs of different populations. Psychologists consult with, refer to, or cooperate with other professionals and institutions to the extent needed to serve the best interests of their patients, clients, or other recipients of their services. Psychologists' moral standards and conduct are personal matters to the same degree as is true for any other person, except as psychologists' conduct may compromise their professional responsibilities or reduce the public's trust in psychology and psychologists. Psychologists are concerned about the ethical compliance of their colleagues' scientific and professional conduct. When appropriate, they consult with colleagues in order to prevent or avoid unethical conduct.

Seven Roads to Trouble

When children experience trouble, parents need to act first as advocates. According to Dr. Haim Ginott, here are seven things parents do which can make the situation where their children find themselves in worse:

1. **Reasoning**
   Example: "So what did you expect? Life's not fair. You have to learn to deal with it."
2. **Clichés**
   "Don't count your chickens before they're hatched. You made your bed, now lie in it. Make a bridge and get over it. Don't cry over spilled milk."
3. **"Take me, for instance."**
   "When I was your age, I walked four miles to school in the snow. I never spoke to my parents that way."
4. **Minimizing the situation**
   "Oh, come on. You'll date lots of girls in the next few years. There are lots of fish in the sea; So you lost your job—jobs at these fast food places are a dime a dozen."
5. **"The trouble with you is. . ."**
   "You go around with a chip on your shoulder. You don't know how to treat a girl. You always talk too much."
6. **Self-pity**
   "My heart breaks for you. Life is so unfair. Other people just have all the luck. It's who you know, they say, and I guess we don't know them!"
7. **A "Pollyana" approach**
   "When a door closes, a window always opens. Everything happens for the best. It was meant to be."

Have you ever heard any of these lines? If so, how did you feel? Have you ever used any of these lines yourself?

Adapted from *Between Parent and Teenager*, by Dr. Haim G. Ginott.

The precepts of the law are these, to live honestly, to injure no one, and to give every person his due.

—Justinian

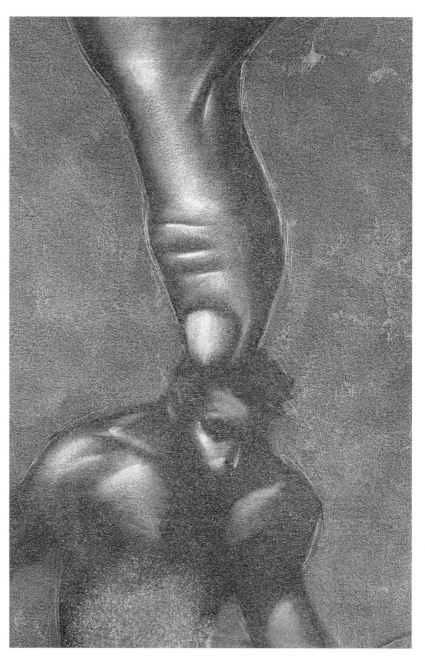

Stress puts pressure on human beings, both physically and emotionally; psychologists can suggest tools for dealing courageously with the stress we all encounter.

6

COURAGE

*Psychologists have no magic answers—but
we can take courage from their work.*

In the 1930s, Canadian endocrinologist Hans Selye began researching
the effects of stress on the body. According to his theory of stress, all
stressors call for adaptation, in which an organism has to regain its balance. Selye discovered that the body's ability to regain balance works
best when the stress is short-lived, but long-term stress can reduce the
ability of the body to fight cancer and other life-threatening infections.
In the presence of chronic stress, the body increases its production of
"stress hormones," which helps us deal with short-term stress but can
actually impair the immune system, with possible long-term negative
health consequences. It may seem, from this research, that disease is
the inevitable response to stress.

Psychologists today, however, know that there is another compo-
nent to the equation: psychological interpretation, or the way in which
people appraise potentially stressful events. Their interpretation of
events may actually change the way their body reacts physiologically,
or the impact its reaction has on their well-being. In other words, to a
certain extent people get to decide how much importance to assign to
each stressor, and their decision may change how their body reacts.

There is still a great deal of information to be learned about
the mind-body connection and illness. For instance, researchers have

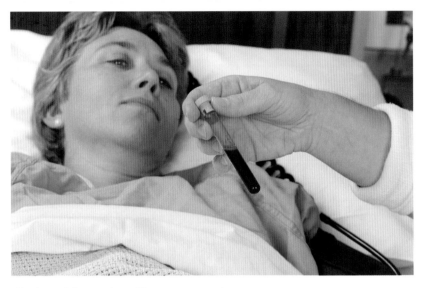

Coping with a serious illness can require great courage.

divided people into personality types, and have discovered that those who actively fight back against cancer may actually fare better in the long run than those who accept the disease passively.

It takes great courage to face life's more difficult stressors, but researchers who study and assess different ways of facing stress provide us with tools that can help us summon that courage from deep inside ourselves. In 1964, *Saturday Review* editor Norman Cousins summoned his courage to fight back against a major illness in a previously unheard-of way. Doctors told Cousins that he had a one in 500 chance of full recovery from a degenerative disease of his body's connective tissue. The diagnosis terrified Cousins, and he wondered

People who value courage:

- say what's right (even when no one agrees with them).
- do the right thing (even when it's hard).
- follow their conscience instead of the crowd.
- keep going in spite of hardship or difficulty.

if his high-stress lifestyle as a magazine editor might not have contributed to his illness.

He read *The Stress of Life*, written by Hans Selye, and reasoned that
if stress could destroy the body, perhaps anti-stress could help rebuild
it. Along with his medical therapy, Cousins devised for himself a regular program of viewing Marx Brothers movies (which he had always
found hilarious) and *Candid Camera* film clips. The more he laughed,
the more his pain and symptoms disappeared, and he eventually recov-
ered. Although Cousins never claimed that laughter alone cured him, he
was emphatic in his support of the idea that positive emotions can enhance the healing process.

Later on, hospitals in Houston, Los Angeles, and Honolulu began
providing videotapes of humorous films to patients, and "laugh wag-
ons" with funny books and tapes are now common in health centers
around the country. Cousins tells of a Catholic hospital in Texas where
the nuns are expected to tell at least one joke a day.

Laughter helps human beings get along better.

Can humor actually give us courage? Are there actual medical benefits to fighting back against disease in this way? Psychologists and other scientists are still studying these issues, but so far we know that:

- In some cases, inflammation can decrease after only a few moments of strong laughter; for Cousins, ten minutes of hearty laughing resulted in two hours of pain-free sleep.
- Laughter has been compared to "stationary jogging," increasing heart rate and oxygenating the blood six times more than ordinary speech.
- Salivary immunoglobulin A, thought to protect the body against some diseases, increases significantly in people who watch funny videos for 30 minutes, and people who say they use humor to deal with difficult life situations have the highest levels of this substance.

Laughter and good times may actually have physical benefits as well as emotional ones.

Courage for Stress

All human beings experience stress. The ability to cope with unavoidable stress is an important skill to be learned. Here are some coping skills psychologists recommend:

1. *Take your time and gather information.*
   Conflict makes us uncomfortable. As a result, we often try to end the conflict as soon as possible, sometimes rushing to make a decision that could compound our problem. Learning to acknowledge and accept our discomfort can help us take time to gather all necessary information about the conflict. Once we get that information, we may find we have tools that make our decision making easier.
2. *Trust in time.*
   Stressful events can cause great pain, and sometimes, despair. When it seems your world has collapsed, remember that studies have shown that people often find new—and equally fulfilling—worlds, if they will just give the situation time.
3. *Stay in contact with other people.*
   Those who are lonely and alone suffer stress more than those who have company. The presence of others can distract you from your pain by keeping you from constant self-reflection.
4. *Think positively and rationally; keep a sense of humor, and put your disappointments in perspective.*
   There are hundreds of ways to be happy. Not all of our original goals are worth meeting. Sigmund Freud said: "Beware of what you really want. You might get it."
5. *Think of yourself as a relaxed person.*
   Begin moving, speaking, and eating more slowly. Take deep breaths and stop periodically to consciously relax your muscles. When you are forced to wait, as in a traffic jam or a doctor's office, put your time to good use by listening to music or bringing along meaningful reading material.

Adapted from *Psychology,* by John P. Dworetzky (St. Paul, Minn.: West, 1992).

What Should We Fear?

Socrates said that courage involved knowing what really is to be feared. He thought of courage as an integral part of virtue, which consists in knowing which things are really good or evil. He believed that if moral evil is the only real evil, then the things we so often call evil (poverty, sickness, suffering, death) are not to be feared; if we face them in the proper spirit, they cannot make us morally worse creatures.

Adapted from *The Book of Virtues*, edited by William J. Bennett (New York: Simon & Schuster, 1997).

Health psychologists continue to study the stress-health relationship from many angles. But results continue to indicate that courage—whether to fight back against a life-threatening illness or to confront our worst fears and secrets by talking them out with trusted friends and advisors—can be very beneficial. Psychologist James Pennebaker's research has demonstrated that holding on to "shameful" secrets, suppressing thoughts and feelings about personal traumas or failures, can undermine our body's defenses against illnesses of both the body and mind. Confiding in other seems to neutralize these negative effects and is often followed by improved physical and psychological health. In other words, psychologists' research and counseling work can help us all find the courage we need to face life's stresses.

One has to go down into what one most fears and in that process . . . comes a saving flicker of light and energy that, even if it does not produce the courage of a hero, at any rate enables a trembling mortal to take one step further.

—Laurens Van Der Post

Being a good school psychologist requires self-discipline and diligence.

7

SELF-DISCIPLINE AND DILIGENCE

When we meet life's challenges . . .
over and over and over . . . we leave
our mark upon the world.

When Dennis Gardner was studying to become a psychologist, he often felt frustrated at all he had to learn, especially when it came to memorizing charts and tables of the developmental stages of human beings. Other psychology students had teased him for working so hard, but once he began his work as school psychologist at the Skyview School District, he found plenty of reasons to be glad for all that work he'd done.

Shannon was one of those reasons. A lanky sixth grader, Shannon seemed to be always on the outside looking in. While the other sixth-grade girls spent lunch time giggling over a new cheer they'd just made up for that afternoon's basketball game, Shannon sat alone and finished her homework.

It wasn't that the girls didn't invite her. They tried—or at least they used to try—but soon gave up when they heard Shannon's invariable reply: "I have to get my homework done now. I have to be at the Conservatory after school."

Everyone knew Shannon spent all her afternoons practicing piano at the Conservatory, preparing for two and sometimes three lessons per week. Shannon was a prodigy. She had won a statewide music contest

A diligent school psychologist takes time to listen to students.

People who value self-discipline and diligence:

- work to control their emotions, words, actions, and impulses.
- give their best in all situations.
- keep going even when the going is rough.
- are determined and patient.
- try again even when they fail the first time.
- look for ways to do their work better.

Adapted from material from the Character Education Network (www.CharacterEd.Net).

back in third grade by playing one of the most difficult of Chopin's compositions, known as the "Black Key Etude," a piece with which even college students usually struggled. Her prize for winning was guaranteed admission and full tuition at the Conservatory after high school, along with special afternoon instruction while she was still in school. Ever since, Shannon had been tagged as a musical genius. Although her parents kept her in public school in hopes that her upbringing would have some semblance of normalcy, everyone knew

Shannon was different. Even the teachers let her off the hook with other homework and projects. "You're so busy with your music, dear," they always said to her, while the other kids made faces and rolled their eyes, angry at the special treatment she received.

Dennis, however, was angry for a different reason. According to Erik Erikson's studies on development, Shannon was still in the "latency stage," the stage that included school children from about six to 12. Dennis knew children of this age needed to develop a capacity for industry, avoid a sense of inferiority, and experience success in some area.

On the other hand, too much industry could lead to a *maladaptive* tendency called "narrow virtuosity," a situation in which a child is not allowed to be a child but is pushed into one area of competence with no opportunity to develop broader interests. Dennis had read all too often about the child actors, child athletes, child musicians, and other prodigies who ended up famous for their accomplishments in one area but without a real life of any kind. Dennis was concerned that this was

Children need a chance to play if they are to develop psychologically.

Erik Erikson is famous for his work on developmental stages of human beings, but other psychologists have also done much work in this area as well. Here are the stages of moral reasoning developed by one psychologist.

Kohlberg's Stages of Moral Reasoning

I. Preconventional morality
Stage 1: Pleasure/pain orientation—to avoid pain or not get caught.
Stage 2: Cost-benefit orientation—to get rewards; reciprocity—an eye for and eye.

II. Conventional morality
Stage 3: Good-child orientation—to gain acceptance and avoid disapproval.
Stage 4: Law and order orientation—to follow rules, avoid censure by authorities.

III. Principled morality
Stage 5: Social contract orientation—to promote the society's welfare.
Stage 6: Ethical principle orientation—to achieve justice and avoid self-condemnation.
Stage 7: Cosmic orientation—to be true to universal principles and feel oneself part of a cosmic direction that transcends social norms.

From *Psychology and Life*, by Philip G. Zimbardo and Richard J. Gerrig (New York: HarperCollins, 1996).

where Shannon might be headed, and he knew he had to get her parents involved. His first step would be to schedule an appointment with Shannon's parents to talk about helping her develop not only as a fine pianist, but as a fine friend and member of her community.

After his phone call to Shannon's parents, Dennis turned to the rest of his schedule for the day. After lunch, he'd be meeting with Katie, a

Self-Discipline and Diligence
(the American Psychiatric Association Ethics Code)

Psychologists strive to maintain high standards of competence in their work. They recognize the boundaries of their particular competencies and the limitations of their expertise. They provide only those services and use only those techniques for which they are qualified by education, training, or experience. Psychologists are cognizant of the fact that the competencies required in serving, teaching, and/or studying groups of people vary with the distinctive characteristics of those groups. . . . They maintain knowledge of relevant scientific and professional information related to the services they render, and they recognize the need for ongoing education. Psychologists make appropriate use of scientific, professional, technical, and administrative resources.

School psychologists work to ensure that each child has a chance at a happy and well-balanced life.

Being a parent is rewarding—but hard work!

sophomore who was six months pregnant and determined to keep her baby. Once again, Dennis would draw on his knowledge of developmental stages, explaining to her how difficult the life of a teenage mother can be. Even though she might be well able to care for her baby physically, Dennis had to help her see that, as a teen, she was still doing the important work of finding out who she was and how she fit into society. Because there was no possibility of the baby's father supporting her either financially or emotionally, Katie would also have to deal with money issues on her own. Later on, much of her energy would probably be used in finding and developing a relationship that offered her intimacy and love. And all the while, her baby would have the simple, straightforward needs all infants have; most important would be the baby's need for a mother with mature abilities and the social support all mothers need. Dennis's job was not to tell Katie what she should do, however. Instead, he would help her understand all her options and their consequences. Then he would offer emotional support, whatever decision she ultimately made.

After meeting with Katie, Dennis and a group of other psychologists would meet with children at an elementary school across town. The afternoon before, a much-loved fourth grade teacher there had been killed in a car accident on her way home from teaching. Dennis and the other psychologists would discuss loss and sadness and grief with the students. Then they would be available for counseling for the rest of the afternoon. Tomorrow, Dennis would help students decide possible career choices by evaluating different tests he had administered the week before.

Dennis loved his work with school students. Though some of his college classmates had teased him for his careful, diligent studying, Dennis was not only glad he'd worked so hard, he planned to keep right on educating himself now by reading journals and attending confer-

---

Five Questions to Ask Everyday

The following five questions, which we can ask ourselves every day, are valuable tools we can use to help us practice the positive character qualities we want to develop:

1. Did I practice any virtues today?
   (Author William Bennett in *The Book of Virtues* says that virtues are "habits of the heart." Virtues include, but are not limited to, integrity, trustworthiness, honesty, and compassion. Virtues are the best parts of ourselves.
2. Did I do more good than harm today?
   (To answer this, you must consider both short-term and long-term consequences.)
3. Did I treat people with dignity and respect today?
4. Was I fair and just today?
5. Was my community better because I was in it?
   (Your "community" can be your neighborhood, family, company, church, etc.)

Material adapted from the Markkula Center for Applied Ethics.

ences. This helped him keep up with the latest research being done in his field, and made him even more of a help to the students and their families.

Being a school psychologist was not an easy or routine job. Each day was different, and no supervisor oversaw Dennis's work every moment of the day. He could have sat in his office shuffling papers—but his own self-discipline and diligence kept him busy every day. The same qualities helped him make a difference in the lives of the young people with whom he worked.

Learning is not attained by chance, it must be sought for with ardor and attended to with diligence.

—Abigail Adams

Voting is just one way to be a good citizen.

8

CITIZENSHIP

*A healthy society depends on each
individual doing his or her part.*

Citizenship is the character quality that binds us together. It is the trait that pushes us to offer each other the best we have to give. If all of us acted as good citizens, our world would be a better place for everyone. Unfortunately, some people act destructively toward others in their community, rather than constructively.

These destructive human behaviors are not always easy to understand. Psychologists observe these behaviors, formulate **hypotheses**, and then collect data to test the validity of their hypotheses. They then apply the knowledge they have gained to help people.

One of the most intriguing and alarming behaviors of the 20th century occurred in 1964, in Queens, New York. One night, a woman named Kitty Genovese was attacked on the street. Kitty fought with her attacker, screaming so loudly that lights came on in apartments overlooking the street, and at least 38 people observed the woman being stabbed. The lights scared off the attacker, but Kitty still lay in the street, wounded. No one came to her aid. One by one, the lights went off, and eventually the attacker came back and stabbed Kitty again. For a second time, he was frightened away by people looking out their windows, but still no one came to her aid. When the lights went out, the attacker returned for a third time. This time, he killed Kitty.

People who value citizenship:

- play by the rules.
- obey the law.
- do their share.
- respect authority.
- stay informed about current events.
- vote.
- protect their neighbors and community.
- pay their taxes.
- give to others in their community who are in need.
- volunteer to help.
- protect the environment.
- conserve natural resources for the future.

Adapted from material from the Character Counts Coalition, 4640 Admiralty Way, Suite 1001, Marina del Rey, California 90292.

In all the time that this horrible situation was taking place, not one onlooker called the police or even an ambulance. This lack of aid was made even more incomprehensible by the fact that the onlookers could have helped Kitty—perhaps saved her life—by simply picking up the phone and making a call. They would not have put themselves in danger; they would not have had to face the attacker. What could explain their lack of action on behalf of Kitty Genovese?

Social psychologists have long observed that sometimes people will go out of their way to help others or prevent them from being hurt. Yet at other times, they will simply refuse to help someone in need. Social psychologists try to determine what factors have an effect on the willingness or unwillingness to help.

Two researchers, Darley and Latane, conducted an experiment in 1968 that may help explain what had happened in Kitty Genovese's situation. They discovered that people are more likely to help others when they are the only ones around to give that help, and are more likely to ignore those in need of help when there are several, or even a few, other people around. This is known as the bystander effect.

Social psychologists have studied the bystander effect, and concluded that there are probably two underlying causes:

1. the ***diffusion of responsibility***
2. fear of appearing foolish

Helping others should be the human norm, learned from our parents when we are very young. Unfortunately, for too many people, this is not the case.

Many psychological studies have been done to determine when an individual is most likely to help others who are in trouble. Researchers Latane and Darley in 1970 described a five-step process people usually must complete before they are likely to give help:

1. The event must be observed.
2. The event must be interpreted as an emergency.
3. The person must accept responsibility for helping.
4. The person has to decide how to help.
5. Action must be taken.

In 1982, when a Boeing 737 took off from Washington D.C.'s National Airport, it crashed into the 14th Street bridge, flipped over, then went through the ice into the Potomac River. Lenny Skutnik, a Washington office worker, went through the process described above this way:

1. He witnessed the disaster on his way home.
2. He saw a rescue helicopter trying to save the drowning crash victims.
3. He noticed that one female victim did not seem to have the strength to hold onto the life preserver that dangled from the helicopter. When Lenny looked around at the others on the bank with him, he realized that "she was going to drown if I didn't go get her, because nobody else was going to."
4. Lenny saw that the only way to reach the woman was to jump into the icy Potomac River and swim to her.
5. He jumped into the river, filled with ice chunks and potentially explosive jet fuel, and saved the woman's life.

Psychologists study what makes some people reach out to others from an early age—and what makes others turn their backs on other's needs.

Psychologists have found that there are at least three important ways of encouraging people to help other people:

1. Studying social psychology and becoming aware of studies on this subject.
2. Teaching appropriate emergency lifesaving skills. (A person who can't swim would be unlikely to jump into a river to rescue a drowning person. A person who has never learned the **Heimlich maneuver** doesn't have the skills to help a choking victim.)
3. Modeling helping behavior and reinforcing others for helping.

Citizenship
(from the American Psychiatric Association's Ethics Code)

Psychologists are aware of their professional and scientific responsibilities to the community and the society in which they work and live. They apply and make public their knowledge of psychology in order to contribute to human welfare. Psychologists are concerned about and work to mitigate the causes of human suffering. When undertaking research, they strive to advance human welfare and the science of psychology. Psychologists try to avoid misuse of their work. Psychologists comply with the law and encourage the development of law and social policy that serve the interests of their patients and clients and the public. They are encouraged to contribute a portion of their professional time for little or no personal advantage.

Studies that help us understand peoples' motivation for helping or not helping in situations such as that of Kitty Genovese are important. The results can be translated into ways to encourage the good citizenship necessary for a healthy society.

The foundations of our national policy will be laid in the pure and immutable principles of private morality.

—George Washington

A psychologist has many opportunities from which to choose.

9

CAREER OPPORTUNITIES

*Seek out the opportunities in life that will
bring you the most fulfillment.*

Susan and Shawn were worried about the fact that their three-year-old daughter Shaundra exhibited little interest in learning to talk. When they discussed the issue with Shaundra's pediatrician, he helped by showing them guidelines for normal language development in children. These guidelines had been established through the work of *developmental psychologists* who had studied how children acquire language.

Lori and Ed were determined to be there for Ed's brother, Kevin, especially now that Kevin's marriage had ended. Ed found it painful to watch his brother struggle with severe depression, but he and Lori were committed to helping, no matter what it took. One way they helped was to make sure that Kevin met with his *clinical psychologist* on a regular basis. The counseling he received there helped Kevin get through this difficult time and go on to rebuild his life.

Charmaine was delighted when she got a promotion to supervisor at the factory where she worked. As a single parent, the raise that went along with the promotion was more than welcome, too. But there was no supervisory training to go along with her new responsibilities, and she soon started to feel that things were getting out of control. The more inefficient Charmaine felt in her new role, the more stress she experienced. Within a few months of her promotion, it was all she could do to

Some psychologists work with couples to help them resolve their differences constructively.

Earnings

Median annual salary for all psychologists (in the 1990s) with:

Doctoral degrees	$55,000
in business & industry	$67,000
federal government	$49,900
Master's degrees	$25,700
Bachelor's degrees	$17,000

Psychologists with doctoral degrees in independent private practice usually have higher earnings than other psychologists. Many supplement their income by consulting, writing, or lecturing.

force herself to get on the bus in the morning to go to work. When Charmaine's boss saw her stress, he insisted that she talk with the *industrial psychologist* who specialized in organizational behavior. With his help, Charmaine was able to develop a plan to get more training and to supervise more efficiently.

When 22-year-old Scott was caught on surveillance cameras at the convenience store robbery, the picture clearly showed the gun in his hand. The police said it would be an "open-and-shut" case, but Scott's mother knew her son had only the intelligence of a five-year-old. She also knew that, while Scott would never by himself think of robbing a store, he would be only too glad to oblige any "friend" who told him to hold the gun. A *forensic psychologist* was called as an expert witness at the trial. She worked with the court to determine Scott's mental competence to stand trial.

Psychologists play important roles in helping our society know and understand itself, and there are many different career opportunities in this field. Jobs for psychologists are projected to grow at an average rate for all occupations through at least 2008. In the area of health care, the fastest growing sector will be outpatient mental health and substance abuse treatment clinics. Management consulting services, and public and private social service agencies will also have job opportunities. School psychologists are expected to have the best job prospects, because schools are expected to increase student mental health services and counseling. Psychologists' expertise in survey design, analysis, and research on marketing evaluation and statistical analysis will be in demand in industry, as will jobs for psychologists who offer company

Psychologists have the exciting opportunity to study what goes on inside the human mind.

Maslow's Hierarchy of Needs

According to psychologist Abraham Maslow all us need more than just money or possessions to be truly happy. The needs listed at the lower level of his hierarchy dominate our motivation as long as they are unsatisfied. When these needs are met, we are free to pursue the higher levels of needs.

Transcendence
spiritual needs for cosmic identification
Self-Actualization
needs to fulfill potential, have meaningful goals
Esthetic
needs for order, beauty
Cognitive
needs for knowledge, understanding, novelty
Esteem
needs for confidence, sense of worth and competence,
self-esteem and respect of others
Attachment
needs to belong, to affiliate, to love and be loved
Safety
needs for security, comfort, tranquility, freedom from fear
Biological
needs for food, water, oxygen, rest, sexual expression,
release from tension

employees assistance with personal problems. Increased interest in providing psychological services for specific groups (such as the elderly or children) will create the possibility of more jobs, as long as government funding is available.

Declining college enrollments are expected to lead to fewer faculty positions for those in this field. Those with doctorates will find the best prospects in all areas of psychology, while competition for jobs among those holding master's degrees is expected to be severe. Graduates with a bachelor's degree will find fewer openings, mostly as assistants in rehabilitation centers, in jobs that involve data collection and analysis, or as high school psychology teachers.

If you choose a career in psychology, you will have opportunities to advance in your profession. But being a psychologist has far deeper possibilities than those offered by any title or salary figure. The opportunity to make the world a better place can't be measured.

Psychologists do not have the answer to all our society's problems. But they are working to help individuals become emotionally healthier and happier. Psychologists have wonderful opportunities. . . to show us all how to live with integrity, respect and compassion, justice and fairness, responsibility, courage, diligence and self-discipline, and citizenship.

Be more concerned with your character than with your reputation. Your character is what you really are while your reputation is merely what others think you are.

—Dale Carnegie

FURTHER READING

Bennett, William J., ed. *The Book of Virtues.* New York: Simon & Schuster, 1997.

Crabb, Larry. *Connecting; Healing for Ourselves and Our Relationships: A Radical New Vision.* Nashville, Tenn.: Word Publishing, 1997.

Dworetzky, John P. *Psychology.* St. Paul, Minn.: West, 1982.

Ginott, Haim G. *Between Parent and Teenager.* Toronto, Ont.: Macmillan, 1996.

Hopke, William E., ed. *The Encyclopedia of Careers and Vocational Guidance,* Ninth Ed. Chicago: J. G. Ferguson, 1993.

Josephson, Michael S. and Wes Hanson, editors. *The Power of Character.* San Francisco: Jossey-Bass, 1998.

Kidder, Rushworth M. *How Good People Make Tough Choices.* New York: Simon & Schuster, 1995.

The U.S. Department of Labor. *Occupational Outlook Handbook, 2001.* Washington, D.C.: U.S. Government Printing Office, 2001.

Zimbardo, Philip G. and Richard J.Gerrig. *Psychology and Life*, 14th Edition. New York: HarperCollins, 1996.

For More Information

American Psychological Association
750 1st Street, NE
Washington, DC 20002
www.apa.org

Association of State and Provincial Psychology Boards
P. O. Box 4389
Montgomery, AL 36103-4389
www.asppb.org

Canadian Psychological Association
Vincent Road
Old Chelsea PQ J0X 2N0

Center for the 4th and 5th Rs
www.cortland.edu/c4n5rs

Character Education Network
www.charactered.net

Josephson Institute of Ethics
www.josephsoninstitute.org

National Association of School Psychologists
8455 Colesville Road
Suite 1000
Silver Spring, MD 20910
www.naspweb.org

National Mental Health Association
1021 Prince Street
Alexandria, VA 22314

Glossary

Ageism Prejudice against older people, similar to sexism and racism in its negative stereotypes.

Alzheimer's disease A degenerative disease of the central nervous system that causes mental deterioration.

Amnesia Loss of memory, usually due to brain injury, shock, or illness.

Behavior modification Set of procedures for changing human behavior, especially by using behavior therapy.

Behavior therapy Manipulation of an individual's behavior to promote adaptive patterns and eliminate maladaptive patterns.

Dementia A condition of deteriorated mental ability.

Deviant Not conforming to normal parameters for acceptable behavior.

Dexterity The ability to use one's hands well.

Diffusion of responsibility The belief, upon seeing someone in need of help in the presence of many people, that one need not act because others probably will.

Heimlich maneuver Using your hands to apply sudden upward pressure on the upper abdomen of a choking victim to force a foreign object from the windpipe.

Hypothesis A theory or guess.

Maladaptive Having behavior that is poorly suited for a particular situation.

Phobia A specific, unrealistic and pathological fear of an object or situation.

Psychoanalysis An insight therapy based on the theory and work of Sigmund Freud.

Psychotherapy Any noninvasive psychological technique designed to bring about a positive change in someone's behavior, personality, or adjustment.

Social learning Learning through observing another's behavior.

Stereotypes Rigid, simplistic, and often untrue ways of thinking about groups of people.

Systematic desensitization A therapeutic procedure pairing anxiety-producing stimuli with a state of physical relaxation, in a graduated sequence, until the most difficult situation can be faced without anxiety.

Transference A tendency of a patient in therapy to transfer to the therapist perceptions and feelings about other people rather than seeing the therapist as he or she really is.

INDEX

American Psychiatric Association 9, 18, 67, 78

American Psychological Association (APA) 9, 12

amnesia 8, 88

behavior modification 8, 88

behavior therapy 5, 88

character 14, 21, 69, 85

deviant behaviors 12

educational requirements 11–12

Erickson, Erik 65, 66

ethics 9, 18, 19, 21, 28, 38, 50, 67, 78

Freud, Sigmund 9, 1, 59

Ginott, Haim 47, 48, 51, 52

hypotheses 73

jobs 11, 12–14, 83–85

Maslow, Abraham 84

phobia 5, 88

Principle of Psychology, The 9

psychoanalysis 9, 11, 88

psychology 8–9, 18, 50, 78

psychotherapy 9, 11, 88

social learning 25–27, 29, 31, 88

specialization 12–14

stress 55–57, 59

systematic desensitization 5, 88

transference 10, 88

Wundt, Wilhelm 9

BIOGRAPHIES

Shirley Brinkerhoff is a writer, editor, speaker, and musician. She graduated Summa Cum Laude from Cornerstone University with a Bachelor of Music degree, and from Western Michigan University with a Master of Music degree. She has published six young adult novels, three nonfiction books for young adults, scores of short stories and articles, and teaches at writers' conferences throughout the United States.

Cheryl Gholar is a Community and Economic Development Educator with the University of Illinois Extension. She has a Ph.D. in Educational Leadership and Policy Studies from Loyola University, and she has more than 20 years of experience with the Chicago Public Schools as a teacher, counselor, guidance coordinator, and administrator. Recognized for her expertise in the field of character education, Dr. Gholar assisted in developing the K–12 Character Education Curriculum for the Chicago Public Schools, and she is a five-year participant in the White House Conference on Character Building for a Democratic and Civil Society. The recipient of numerous awards, she is also the author of *Beyond Rhetoric and Rainbows: A Journey to the Place Where Learning Lives.*

Ernestine G. Riggs is an Assistant Professor at Loyola University Chicago and a Senior Program Consultant for the North Central Regional Educational Laboratory. She has a Ph.D. in Educational Leadership and Policy Studies from Loyola University, and she has been involved in the field of education for more than 35 years. An advocate of teaching the whole child, she is a frequent presenter at district and national conferences; she also serves as a consultant for several state boards of education. Dr. Riggs has received many citations, including an award from the United States Department of Defense Overseas Schools for Outstanding Elementary Teacher of America.